This book is dedicated to **YOU!**
Whether you purchased it, received it as a gift, or
borrowed it – it found you and you found it for good
reason. There is no such thing as a coincidence or
happenstance. Trust those moments of magic and turn
them into your most desired riches.

–Roger L. Brooks

Table of Contents

THE POWER OF BEING RICH

10 Essential Principles to Manifest What You Already Have

Introduction

What can you expect from this book?

Transparency. I will pass along everything I've learned and everything I know about The Power of Being Rich. I will demonstrate how I've been able to manifest the amazing riches into my life. By reading this book, you will have a greater appreciation and respect for your own ability to tap into your internal riches. And if you put some of these tools into practice, you will vibrate at a higher frequency and the doors to your world will begin to open in abundance. You must be willing, however, to put in the work and make conscious decisions to better yourself so you can better your life.

This book is as much about the philosophy of mindset as it is about the mechanics of becoming rich. Yes, there are tools to help you become rich, but what will set you apart? What will be unique about *your* identity and *your* reality that attracts riches to you and you to your riches?

Breaking through the clutter of the mind is not easy. It takes discipline and practice to form new habits. The good news is that it can be learned. Once you turn the clutter off, it's disconnected, just as you disconnect a plug from an outlet, and it will not reconnect unless you consciously choose to do so.

Too many people wander through life aimlessly, looking for answers. They're reactive, not proactive, waiting for things to "just happen" to them because they feel it's owed, they're entitled, or that they've earned the right.

But how can you break through all the chatter? How can you wrap your arms and your mind around this new way of thinking? And how can you get on the path towards *The Power of Being Rich*?

I have taken more than 30 years of life experience and experimentation and put it into this book. If there's one thing I've learned it's this: if you have trust in yourself, trust the process of the principles outlined in this book and act in a specific way, you most certainly will become rich. However, YOU and ONLY YOU hold the keys!

You will be the difference. You, in all of your authentic glory and splendor. You uncovering your uniqueness. You demonstrating your vulnerability. You being transparent – as much to yourself as to the world. It is ALL up to YOU.

If you believe you can't get this part right, then stop reading now. The first step is believing. Believe in YOUR dream for YOU and YOUR family.

What will follow on these pages is only intended for those who are open and ready to look at their reality with a new lens. It's the only way to form your new reality. You must not only be ready but willing to embrace your new reality with all of your being. You must be ready to get aggressive by taking action, while remaining humble.

Ready to stand in confidence, yet able to put your ego aside, forever. Ready to give more than you receive. Ready to do it, not for the fame or fortune, but for the impact you will make on the world. Ready to inspire, empower, and enlighten all those you touch every single day.

It doesn't matter where you come from. It doesn't matter what your financial status may be. It doesn't matter what environment or circumstances you're in. It doesn't matter what rank you've attained, or where you are in your career. It doesn't matter what you've already achieved, or are yet to achieve.

The only thing that truly matters is that you have a burning desire deep within yourself to become the very best version of yourself. Above all, you must have faith. Faith in YOU and faith in a higher source that wants nothing more than for you to advance and increase and live in the abundance that is rightfully yours for the taking.

Acknowledgments

This book would not be possible without the many mentors I've embraced over the course of my life. I will name them in chronological order as they were introduced into my life.

Thank you, God.

Denis Waitley, Jeffrey Gitomer, Earl Nightingale, Saint Francis of Assisi, Gary Vaynerchuk, Brian Rose, David Neagle, Wallace Wattles, Ed Mylett and David Meltzer.

I am grateful for my wife, Sabrina; our children, Alexis and Roger II; my parents, Roger and Nancy; my mother-in-law, Rosetta; my sister, Stephanie, and her husband, Steve, and their children, Sophia and Maia, and my sister-in-law, Romina, and her husband, Ray, and their children, Ray IV (and Maddie), Gabriella (and Walter), Julia, and Maximus. Thank you all for who you are and what you do to bring joy into my life.

A special thanks to Andre Haykal, Jr., who held me accountable in completing this book and is my *young* teacher.

I'd like to thank Martin Bidney, Professor Emeritus, Binghamton University for taking the time to edit this book while he's currently working to finalize his 28th book of poetry.

Chapter 1
Manifest Your Reality

WHATEVER YOU TRULY DESIRE, OR WISH FOR, IS ALREADY THERE.

A Reality in Limbo. What reality are you living in?

For most of my life, I've lived in fear... a fear-based reality, that is. Fear of who I wasn't. Fear of what I didn't know. Fear of what I didn't have. Fear of what I wouldn't accomplish. Fear of being rejected. Fear of not being liked. Fear of not fitting in. Fear of not being successful. But more than anything, I didn't have a good sense of *me*, and therefore I did not have a good sense of my reality. My biggest fear, quite frankly, was not knowing my identity. I did not know who I was supposed to be, or who I should show up as to the world.

Hence, my life had become an unknown reality, and one that I seemingly had little control over. Before I woke up from my false reality, life was filled with ups and downs and much in between. It was a reality many people can likely relate to. It was a *reality in limbo*.

The challenge with this? Your identity is everything. Your entire interactive life; your thoughts, the way you project yourself to the world and the action you take all stem from your identity. If you don't have a solid understanding of who you are, and can't identify with your internal pureness, it will impact every single area of your life.

So I ask... tell me about yourself — who are you?

I'm not asking what you do for a living, or who your significant other is, I'm asking: what identifies you as you? What is your unique ability? What makes you different from everyone else? What traits and gifts do you have that provide fulfillment and allow you to contribute to the world? What is your TRUE IDENTITY? It's not a question you have to answer now, but it's something you should begin to ponder. Write down your unique qualities. Begin to think about what makes you special. What is your distinct thumbprint that sets you apart from everyone else?

> You are not the child of…
> You are not the friend of…
> You are not the parent of…
> You are not the sibling of…
> You are not the spouse of...
> You are not your job title of...
> **You are your unique YOU!**

So what is this new *genuine* reality I've been living more recently? That's a question I will answer for you throughout this entire book. It's a reality that found me, much as this book found you.

Although I didn't know it at the time, I was first introduced to my new reality by my cousin, Buster Fiacco, back in the 1980s. Buster began his career as an auto mechanic and quickly worked his way up to being the service manager at Ken Wilson Chevrolet. For a side job, he had a snowplow on his truck and serviced a handful of clients to clear their parking lots whenever it snowed in upstate New York. On occasion, Buster would ask if I wanted to tag along. We would eat snacks, have brother-like conversations, and he would sometimes plug in a cassette tape of a motivational speaker. The one that stands out is Denis Waitley. I found the tapes interesting. So much so, that Buster gave me the entire collection. It was called *The Psychology of Winning* and it set me on a path to building a positive mindset.

"THERE ARE TWO PRIMARY CHOICES IN LIFE: TO ACCEPT CONDITIONS AS THEY EXIST, OR ACCEPT THE RESPONSIBILITY FOR CHANGING THEM."

—DENIS WAITLEY

Over time, I found out that this reality I had stumbled upon is a reality many people are living intentionally. It's not something that's typically taught in school, or at home. And it's a reality that everyone *can* live if they're open to it, and are given the tools and the information for that openness, that way of living.

So let's jump in.

It all starts with awareness.

After my introduction to Denis Waitley, my mindset began to shift. By now it was the early 1990s and I had moved to the Pacific Northwest. Portland, Oregon was my destination. I was in my third year of college, but while in school I also put into practice my entrepreneurial drive. I started creating t-shirt designs and eventually started my own clothing line, *Roger Brooks Wear*. I created high quality garments and sold my product to companies like Nordstrom. The problem was I didn't fully appreciate or value the opportunity that was in front of me. Then orders got bigger, and so did the setbacks. And more than anything, I didn't plan for the Portland Trailblazers to send a cease and desist demand letter to the retailers carrying my design, RIP CITY USA. The Blazers claimed they owned the trademark to the name, which they relinquished several weeks later. Then, a wealthy twenty-something decided to copy my work and instead of putting up a fight, I gave up. I had a small stint working with Clyde Drexler and his agent, but it was short-lived. I made plenty of mistakes. There was a ton of resistance, but more than anything, I didn't ask for help. Within a year's time, the company was defunct. I then met my beautiful future bride Sabrina, and for the next fifteen years I worked with my brother-in-law Ray, helping to build, grow and sell two of his businesses. It was a lot of fun, and I learned a tremendous amount about business.

Then, in 2008, Ray introduced me to a book called *The Little Red Book of Selling* by Jeffrey Gitomer. That book began to re-open some of the very same thoughts I had many years before while listening to Denis Waitley. Then, that same year, Ray sent me to Jeffrey Gitomer's Sales Boot Camp in St. Pete Beach, Florida – and that weekend, everything changed.

Jeffrey Gitomer is considered the "King of Sales" and at that time he had written a half-dozen books, all dealing with sales and the sales mindset. His style, persona and passion were all driven by one thing – HIMSELF and his unique abilities, all freely developed while he remained comfortable in his own skin. There was one thing for certain that Jeffrey knew and that was *his* identity.

Throughout the weekend-long event, I became laser-focused on the fact that he simply communicates as himself. His confidence permeated his every word. His writing style is exactly the way he speaks. His delivery from the stage of a crowded room is exactly the way he interacts one-on-one. Jeffrey Gitomer is Jeffrey Gitomer. And Jeffrey being Jeffrey was exactly the wake-up call I needed.

In my downtime that weekend, I was fixated on asking myself one question: *Who are you? Who is Roger Brooks?*

The challenge I had was that I couldn't answer the question. The only thing that came to mind was who I wanted to be, not who I was at my core. But one thing was clear to me that day. I clearly knew I wasn't LIVING as my true and authentic self.

Throughout the seminar, Jeffrey provided examples and told stories about how he had excelled in the sales world as a young man. He began his sales career in the manufacturing business, selling bean-bag chairs in New York City. He described the time as his *comeuppance* in sales. During this period, Jeffrey and a pack of friends drove from New Jersey to New York City. Each day while driving, they'd read a chapter from Napoleon Hill's book, *Think and Grow Rich.* Their reading of Napoleon Hill soon became a habit and they began putting into practice what they read. Later, they expanded their library of self-help resources and started watching a motivational video by Glenn Turner called, *Challenge to America.* Then, they began listening to a popular audiotape, *The Strangest Secret,* by Earl Nightingale. Jeffrey emphasized the impact *The Strangest Secret* made on his life, so I made a note of that and it quickly went to the top of my list.

There were many sales tools, concepts and ideas that came out of the seminar that weekend. I took many notes, purchased a few of Jeffrey's books, and was certainly armed with an abundance of new ideas, sales knowledge, and information. I vividly recall three things that stood out for me as my main takeaways that weekend:

I made a commitment to write my own book.

I would research Earl Nightingale and listen to *The Strangest Secret*.

I would start on my journey to FIND MYSELF.

That weekend was my initiation for learning the fundamentals of professional sales, but it was also my re-introduction to a positive mindset and awareness—something I had ignored for several years. All of a sudden I became more aware of my surroundings, and – what mattered most – I became more aware of my reality and the reality I could ultimately create.

My Journey to Manifesting My Own Reality

Upon my return home, and without knowing it, I would begin my journey of manifestation, of manifesting my own reality. Immediately, I ordered *The Strangest Secret* on audio CD, as YouTube was just making its way to the world. After about a week, the package arrived in the mail and I couldn't wait to play the CD.

Earl Nightingale's creation of *The Strangest Secret* is a work of art and creative genius. He recorded himself reading the powerful text of what he referred to as *the strangest secret in the world*. Although the premise of his message is predicated on uncovering the secret of success, the underlying message is a guide on how to manifest your own reality.

After Nightingale defines success and describes the importance of setting goals, he dives into the main premise of his teaching, *We Become What We Think About* — which he calls *The Strangest Secret in the World*. If you haven't listened to *The Strangest Secret*, I suggest you take a listen now. If you heard it before, listen to it again – and when you do, come at it from a standpoint of pure awareness, remaining laser-focused on Nightingale's words.

There are a few items that stand out for me each time I listen to *The Strangest Secret*.

- The idea of being able to plant a seed in your mind has been around throughout the ages.

- Much of what he says goes back to basic life lessons based on the laws of the universe. Like gravity, these laws are inflexible.

- Going after your goals and dreams comes down to consistency. A thought becomes an idea implemented into action. You first have to see your goal to truly believe in whatever you set out to do, then keep your goal constant and consistent.

For the first time, I began to understand the power we have within — the power of our mind and being able to match that up with the desires within our heart in order to accomplish whatever it is we set out to do.

We Become What We Think About.

The more I listened to the *The Strangest Secret*, the more I began to believe in myself and my abilities and to understand how I could literally manifest whatever it was I set out to do. I quickly found out that the laws of the universe and the power of manifestation can only expand and make available what you are actually capable of and ready to receive. For example, if all you do is try to manifest being successful or being rich, but constantly think about what you don't have, nothing will occur. By contrast, if you are providing a product or service of extreme value and you go at it with a pure heart, putting your entire being into it, and wish to become rich from the value you are providing, you will surely become rich.

Here's an excerpt from Earl Nightingale's *The Strangest Secret*:

Do you want to excel at your particular job? Do you want to go places in your company, in your community? Do you want to get rich? All you have got to do is plant that seed in your mind, care for it, work steadily toward your goal, and it will become a reality. It not only will, there's no way that it cannot. You see, that's a law — like the laws of Sir Isaac Newton, the laws of gravity. If you get on top of a building and jump off, you'll always go down — you'll never go up. And it's the same with all the other laws of nature. They always work. They're inflexible. (Original LP record, 1957, side 2)

Once I learned and believed this lesson, it changed everything for me. In fact, it is a lesson I replicate in my mind over and over again. These laws, the laws of the universe, work one hundred percent of the time and they are TRULY inflexible. In Chapter 7 I will go deeper into the universal laws.

If you stray from your desired reality, it too will stray from you.

My Wake Up Call

We are creatures of habit and, as Nightingale explains, our minds cannot distinguish between success and failure. If we feed our mind thoughts of success, it will return what we plant, but if we feed our mind thoughts of failure, it will return failure just as readily.

I have experience with both success and failure. On my way up the success ladder, I became obsessed with feeding my mind constant reinforcement of positive influence and energy, whether from Earl Nightingale, Napoleon Hill, Dr. Wayne Dyer, Bob Proctor, or Joseph Campbell. I've read or listened to them all. I became obsessed with feeding my mind positive thoughts on an everyday basis.

Then, suddenly I found myself at the height of my career… or so I thought. The company I worked for was acquired, I had a small piece of ownership, and my bank account carried a balance higher than ever before. That is great, right!? It's great if there's a goal, a plan, or even an appreciation. I HAD NONE.

Slowly, I went back to my old ways. I had stopped planting positive daily thoughts of greatness or success into my mind. Instead, I went the opposite way. I had made it big, right? So surely the riches would continue. I continued to enjoy life, buying things for people, always picking up the tab – acting like my bank account was limitless, when in fact it was not, and I knew that.

Then I went through a period of self-doubt, worry and fear – and slowly that's what came back into my world… my old reality. All the hard work of creating my *new* reality slowly disappeared. Although I probably knew the solution, I got into a funk and couldn't get out. Over a couple of years my world began to close in on me and everything I had worked so hard to achieve collapsed in front of my eyes.

But my real secret is this: nobody knew. I told no one.

I hid it from my wife, my immediate family, and my friends. I begged and borrowed financially to cover up what I had lost. I went into a spiral of self-pity and didn't want to admit I needed help. Nor did I ask for it. Not asking for help was the single biggest mistake of my life. I blamed everyone but me.

My lesson out of that entire experience is this:

NEVER let your guard down.
NEVER take your eye off the ball.
NEVER lose sight of your aiming point.
NEVER stop planting seeds of positive intention – every single day.

More than anything, I had to bring back the awareness I had lost… the one that Gitomer helped me gain. I had to become that young, hungry salesman again.

As I write these words, I'm here to tell you it doesn't matter where you feel you are in life. You can change your reality the moment you decide to do so. I am living proof. A rich man can lose everything he has and if he changes his mindset he can once again become rich; however, it takes work, lots of work. Day after day, week after week, month after month. After a couple of years of relentless work, I've once again been able to create my own reality and manifest what I know is already there. Doors begin to open, and opportunity begins to present itself. I've once again found my true self and I've once again been able to create my own reality.

This, friends, is being rich. Being able to create your own reality is the only true form of richness. You can have all of the money in the world, but if you're not happy, you're not rich. And if you're not complete or fulfilled, you're still living a reality in limbo.

Now, begin to think about the reality you want to create. Is it working within your true passion? Is it creating a better home life for you and your family? Is it being more present and serving others first? Is it being more intentional in everything you do? Is it being aware of your thoughts and actions? Is it truly finding your identity and being comfortable in your own skin? Is it all of the above?

Think about it, dream about it. Believe it and live it.

Be the person *you* want to be. Act the part *you* want to play. Be selective about whom you let into *your* reality. Don't hide it. Don't fear it. Speak it, confidently. That is WHO you are. That's your true identity.

"We become what we think about all day long."

—Earl Nightingale

YOUR ABUNDANCE OF RICHES IS ONLY THAT IN WHICH YOU WILL ALLOW YOURSELF TO BELIEVE.

Every person on the planet owns riches from within. They are the instinctive characteristics and traits that are there for the taking, waiting for you to tap into their source. They are the foundational roots of happiness, fulfillment, aspiration — and all that accompanies them. The big question is How do you tap into the existence of internal wealth if it's not naturally there? How do you access pure happiness? How do you find the deep riches from within?

The most important step is to realize what NOT to do in order to keep a clean and clear mind. You must begin to create new habits, and new habits aren't acquired overnight. In fact, it is scientifically proven that it takes 21 days of consistent behavior to form a new habit and it takes three cycles of 21 days each to form a permanent habit. Admittedly, I am not professionally trained in habit formulation. I am simply revealing to you what I've learned, to shed light on how I've lived. Your experience may vary.

Here are SEVEN pre-qualifying steps to begin to find your inner riches:

1. Rid your mind of negative thoughts and don't participate in negative discussion.

2. Don't judge yourself or others. It's okay to observe, but don't pass judgment.

3. Don't play the victim. You are not a victim of circumstance. You create your own circumstances.

4. Eliminate all excuses and take extreme ownership of your actions. Stop relying on other people to get things done.

5. Lose all thoughts of fear. It's easier said than done, but it may be the most important of all. Any time fear creeps in, wipe it out immediately with a positive thought.

6. Banish feelings of guilt and shame. These feelings are deep-rooted and may require the most intense effort to expel from your thoughts.

7. Don't beat yourself up. If you do anything you more recently would have wished to avoid, simply forget it, move on, and get back on track.

When you start to eliminate these negative habits, your focus will begin to shift and your new thoughts will be laser-focused and centered on your newly created reality.

The best analogy I ever heard for the nature of our mind was from Earl Nightingale. He explained that the mind is like a farm. The farmer begins by planning for the crop, readying the tools for planting, and making sure the soil is rich and pure. In the spring, after preparing the crop, and nurturing the crop, the farmer finds the field ready to accept whatever seed is to be sown. The soil never cares what type of seed it gets. You can plant a seed of corn, or you can plant a seed of poisonous nightshade. Then, as long as you continue to care for that seed, it will begin to grow. You must water it, look after it, and be with it each day to ensure it will flourish. If you do all those things, the farm will return an abundant crop – whether of corn or of nightshade.

Our minds respond in the same way. If you feed your mind good and positive thoughts – if you care for it, if you maintain its goodness – it will return goodness to you. On the other hand, if you feed your mind negative thoughts, negative images, negative information, judgment, fear, chaos… it will return the same. As with the field, the mind does not care.

How are you caring for and feeding your mind? Are you feeding it a good wholesome crop of thoughts, images, dreams, aspirations, riches — or are you feeding your mind poison? As Nightingale says, "It's up to you to decide." You have the free will to choose to feed your mind whatever you wish. You have the free will to choose when you will begin and there's no better time than the present.

Optimism and attitude are the key drivers for manifesting your own reality.

Now that you're aware of what not to do and what to eliminate, you can start to focus on what positive actions to take. All the pointers in this book are tools to assist you on your journey. People differ greatly, so you'll want to adopt your own methods and strategies that work for you in implementing your desired reality. When thinking about your riches within, let's break down two key components that are 100% within your control:

- Optimism
- Attitude

Optimism

Optimistic people have a genuine zest for life. It's an underlying characteristic that creates mass appeal for attracting overall goodness. Optimism should not be forced. It's a characteristic that should come naturally based on your general outlook toward yourself, toward others, and toward the life you choose to lead. It's an energy that has the capacity to change the mood of any conversation and can impact all those you encounter. It can be the reason you land that new job, get that raise, land that sale, close that contract, or are granted that date. Being optimistic has ripple effects beyond comprehension and belief, but it starts only when you put it into practice.

Each day when you wake up, you make a choice (conscious or not) of how you will set the tone for the day. Will it be a good day, a bad day, a rough day, a happy day? It's a decision you, and only you can make.

One thing is for certain. Each day is a new day and in order to shape it effectively, you have to guide your thoughts with optimistic intent. Begin to declare that intention and speak it aloud. "Today is a new day. Today, good things will happen because I am in control of my thoughts. Today, positive energy flows to me and through me, and I return that energy to all those I encounter. I have only good intentions today and I will eliminate anything negative from my mind. No one, nothing, can sway me from having thoughts of goodness."

Setting the tone for the day is a practice. As with everything we discuss in this book, practice is the only way to succeed. Practice is the only way to get rich. When you practice optimistic thoughts with positive intention, you will take on the form of that intention and it will become a natural extension of you.

Remember the analogy of the farmer. Every day you must plant those seeds, care for them and nurture them, and they will prosper and grow into an amazing source of goodness.

Have you ever looked at someone and said:

"Why are they always in a good mood?"
"Why are they always in a bad mood?"
"Why are they so happy?"
"Why are they always unhappy?"

Our mood, or our aura, is energy. Tenseness, anger, fear, doubt, and worry all give off a negative energy. Distress can be read on someone's face, just as easily as you can read happiness, cheerfulness, victory, confidence, and tolerance. Our expression is our energy, and our energy is our expression.

Optimism is an energy. Optimistic people give off a strong and positive vibe. By the way people carry themselves, you can tell if they have an optimistic attitude.

Conversely, pessimism is also an energy, and pessimistic people give off a strongly negative vibe. For this type of energy, disruptive and distracting, the pessimist pays a high price. Pessimism will badly affect friendships, relationships, and the prospects for generating good will. A powerful blocking up of mental energy, pessimism overpowers your ability to connect with the source of your riches within.

What type of energy do you exude? Hopefully it is optimism, in every sense of the word. But whatever it is, you have the power to change that energy so that it rises to a higher optimistic frequency. Whether you're pessimistic, somewhat pessimistic, optimistic, or somewhat optimistic, you have full control to raise your level of optimism to a place you might not have thought was possible. The beauty is, optimism builds over time, but never reaches its peak. Why? Because life is not all roses. Adverse events occur: death, loss, setbacks, decisions that do not always go your way. But in hard times you must lift yourself up, rise above them, and take much of the personal emotion out of the loss. It is not our right to influence or be influenced by anything outside ourselves. Leave that to a higher power. Optimism carries momentum! – and that momentum will build every day if you let it do so and if you trust the process.

You have the capacity within you not only to change your energy but literally to change the energy of others. You don't need to talk about it, you don't need to point it out, and you don't need to force it. Your positive energy will have an effect on others by you being you. People will start to take notice. You'll receive comments from others such as, "Something is different about you." They WILL feel your energy shift and it is contagious. You can single-handedly change the energy of another person, or an entire room of people, simply by the energy you emit.

OPTIMISM LIVES DIRECTLY WITHIN YOU, AND YOU CONTROL ITS TEMPO.

I was with David Meltzer, one of my mentors, recently in California. He was offering tips about how he prepares his mind to constantly stay optimistic, filled with an incredible force of energy. He explained that every day he carries with him a large bottle of water, containing an exclusive ingredient available only to those fortunate enough to be told of it. Every sip of water he drinks fills his body with a sensational agent of power. This agent keeps his body young and strong. This agent keeps his mind sharp and focused. This agent keeps his mood uplifted and his tempo high. And this agent gives off an ultraviolet light source that draws others into his thriving force of energy.

Meltzer's water, the ultimate potion, is available to each one of you at this very moment.

Since that day, I too have been drinking the potion. I have bottled it and even allow it into my coffee, or tea. And it's now contained in every liquid I drink. By reading this you too have FULL access to the potion. You now have the right and the knowledge to accept the most wondrous potion known to man. With each sip you will be energized and fulfilled. You ARE optimism.

They may forget what you said, but they will never forget how you made them feel.

—Carl W. Buehner

Attitude

From the time I was young, my parents would say, "Change your attitude, young man." Those words and their voices are still clearly audible in my mind. Looking back, that parental discipline certainly made an impact on me. Our attitude is our spirit and our fortitude. It is everything.

For as long as I can remember, I've wanted to make an impact or impression to improve how I made people feel. My thought process hasn't been anything more than for people to know I'm a good person with good intentions. I've made it a point to be respectful, responsible, and trustworthy. This, felt wholeheartedly, is the sole reason I have had success in my personal and professional life. There's no better feeling than making someone feel good, as long as the feeling is genuine and not gratuitous.

"I love that tie."
"You look great today."
"Where did you get those shoes?"
"You must be doing something right, because your kids are sensational."

Make people feel good. Make people feel comfortable. Listen to people when they speak. Acknowledge their contributions. As David Meltzer says, "Be more interested than interesting."

Start to take the focus off of yourself. Show a general interest in others. Ask questions. Be inquisitive. Have an open mind. Again, be the light and leave everyone you touch with a feeling, not a thought.

If you struggle with maintaining a positive attitude, you're not alone. Society has set us up for failure. The news is filled with negative stories. Conversations are often unproductive, consumed with gossip, repeating negative information.

"OMG, did you hear about Doug?"
"Can you believe they bought another new car?"
"What is with that girl anyway? I hope she rots in Hell."

You get my point. We hear these types of comments, and most people are guilty by participating, or at least guilty by association. That type of discussion or commentary often leads to fueling negative energy. It's important to remain aware of these situations and counteract them whenever possible by simply changing the subject, or at least not feeding into or fueling the fire. Extinguish it and move on.

The power of a smile

Each of you holds the greatest asset to generate a positive attitude. The smile. There's nothing that breaks the ice, opens a conversation, or delivers positive energy more than the sight of an honest smile. Think about how an inviting smile changes the chemistry of any encounter in any situation, any conversation. You can even use a smile in those awkward conversations of gossip. Try it. Instead of participating in any response at all, simply return a smile. You will see that nine times out of ten it will dismiss the negative dialogue. The person will understand it's not something you want to participate in. Non-engagement will send the needed message about where you stand.

Practice your smile. In fact, take a moment right now and smile. Does it not give you an inner feeling of love and happiness? Now the remarkable thing is that the same feeling you have within is what's transmitted out toward others. A smile opens the door to endless possibility. A smile is the alpha and the omega, the beginning and the end. Start each day with a smile, and end each day with a smile. It sets the tone for the day, and it initiates the dialogue for your dreams.

A SMILE OPENS THE DOOR TO ENDLESS POSSIBILITY.

Change Your Attitude!

Right before Labor Day weekend 2018, I had the opportunity to interview David Neagle on my podcast. He's a best-selling author, speaker and host of *The Successful Mind Podcast*. For nearly three decades, David has been teaching people how to improve their mindset, as well as to better understand the laws of the universe. He has success story after success story of people he's helped to make changes within their mindset that forged change in virtually every part of their life, including their income. He has a very pragmatic approach to his message, and it's also his company tagline, *Just Believe.*

In the interview, I asked David if he had an *Aha!* moment, or if there was a breakthrough that took place, helping the forklift driver become a multi-millionaire. He said there absolutely was – and here's how he described it.

"It was a Tuesday night, it was in February, it was freezing cold, I was exhausted and I was in the back of a trailer and I literally had a meltdown. I was just crying, I was angry, I wanted to just break stuff... because I was so frustrated about where I was. And then, suddenly a voice inside my head said, 'change your attitude.' Now I don't know where it came from, but I'm telling you, as God's truth, that's what happened. A voice said, 'change your attitude,' so that's where it started. It was like somebody grabbed me by the neck and said, 'pay attention to this...

pay attention.' And when I changed it, thirty days later I went from making $20,000 a year to the equivalent of $62,000 a year... in thirty days. But this wasn't supposed to happen. I had no education, I had a poor work record, I had no business experience, nothing. And here I was making more money than anybody that I actually even knew was making at that time. And I thought, I have to figure out what I just did... I knew it wasn't luck, I didn't believe in luck. I knew that I had done something, that I had interacted with something that caused this change to happen. And if I could figure that out, I could fulfill the promise that I made when I was hanging from the tree when I got sucked through the dam. When I got sucked through the dam, I went down river and around an island and there was a tree branch hanging in the water. It was the only thing I was able to grab onto because I couldn't get to shore. And when I was hanging on that tree branch, I said one of those bargaining prayers to God. I said, 'If you'll let me live today, I'll figure out why I haven't done what I was supposed to do and then I'll spend the rest of my life teaching other people to do that.' Now, I thought about it over the years... and that was thirty years ago, so I don't know where that came from. At that moment, two things happened. I had an incredible sense of peace that came over me and I was brutally honest with myself. And it wasn't that I didn't know what to do, it was I couldn't figure out how to get myself to do it. So... that was the honesty that hit me in that moment. And then, the culmination of what happened in the trailer that night when it said, 'change your attitude' and then when I saw the result, that gave me the impetus and desire to figure out what caused this. So that put me on a journey of studying for seven years, until I figured out what it was, and ever since then, that's what I've been doing."

A powerful story, from a powerful man who not only changed his attitude, but took complete responsibility, extreme ownership, and didn't play the victim. David learned that his environment wasn't going to change; rather, he needed to change the environment of his mindset... his attitude, in order to have the outcome he desired.

"A VOICE IN MY HEAD SAID, 'CHANGE YOUR ATTITUDE.'"

—DAVID NEAGLE

Chapter 3
Procrastination, Conformity, & Resistance

Take extreme

ownership!

Procrastination

Ever procrastinate, or not follow through on a promise? Ever make up an excuse? Ever had thoughts to improve your stature, influence, or personal brand, but didn't see it through?

Of course you have – everyone has at one point or another. But then, for most, complacency sets in. Either in the form of fear, or by talking yourself out of something. You procrastinate and get comfortable. You get comfortable in your mind, comfortable in your job, and comfortable in life. You'd rather not take on more responsibility because it will be more work. Sound familiar?

What about building your own website, writing a book, starting a podcast, or stepping out of your comfort zone to do something that felt right within your gut and within your heart? You'd like to do some of these things, yet procrastination sets in.

How do you justify *not* progressing? How do you justify *not* investing in yourself? In order to grow your riches, you should be exhausting all avenues for personal growth. Are you observing and researching what the leaders in your field are doing to elevate their game? Or are you still watching TV in the evenings when you should be getting ready for what's on tap for tomorrow? Are you "pressured" to go out with friends more than you should? And are you "working" in your job, but just going through the motions?

These are all conditions, not dilemmas. They are indicators of the fact that those who procrastinate are not taking responsibility for their actions. They are reminders that they're likely not in self-starter mode, or currently don't have the self-motivating tools to make things happen. They're procrastinating.

Do you want to know what to do about it? Do you want to know a sure way of making certain you attain your goals, make the money, and satisfy all of your personal desires?

Of course you do, so let me give you the answer: TAKE EXTREME OWNERSHIP!

Take extreme ownership!

While studying under Brian Rose at the London Real Academy, I learned the true definition of extreme ownership. I say true definition because even though I'd heard the expression before, I didn't appreciate its meaning. Brian passed the expression down to the class from Jocko Willink, a former Navy Seal and guest on *London Real TV*.

In the book, *Extreme Ownership: How U.S. Navy SEALs Lead and Win*, by Jocko Willink and Leif Babin, Willink outlines the epitome of extreme ownership through various scenarios played out on the real-world battlefield.

In chapter 1, Willink explains that while in Ramadi, Iraq, his commanding unit was involved in a blue-on-blue — a friendly fire battle — where U.S. troops inadvertently fired their weapons on friendly forces. One of the friendly forces was killed and several wounded. It was the worst situation Willink had ever encountered. How would he explain? Who was to take the blame? Who would take full responsibility?

Willink had only hours to examine the facts before the investigating officer, the commanding officer, and the command master chief would be there to demand the debriefing. Willink attempted to retrace and reconstruct the mishap and in the process uncovered several gaps, feeling something was missing that he couldn't quite explain. There were various factors, variables, and irregularities in what had occurred, yet he couldn't logically place the blame on one or more individuals for the entire casualty.

What would he do?

Finally, it came time to give the debriefing to his superiors. They wanted answers and demanded to know who was responsible. What Willink did next was unprecedented. As the commander responsible for the entire operation, he took full accountability. He took full responsibility for every action that took place with the friendly fire.

He took **extreme ownership!**

It's remarkable what occurs when you take extreme ownership. There's no more looking around. There's no more finger pointing. There's no more blame. There's no more gossip. There's no more ill-will. There's no more passing the buck. There's no more negative energy toward others. There's no more procrastination, and there are no more excuses.

The only finger-pointing is from the person looking back at you in the mirror.

This made me start to realize that everything inside my mind, whether taught or learned, has been backwards. For my entire life, my thoughts, and what my mind believed to be correct, have been wrong. My own advice, wrong. My instincts, wrong.

But why? Is it just me?

No.

It's because we've been conditioned. It's because we've been taught to follow stereotypes. It's because we've been shaped to do the norm.

As good stewards, we've been conditioned to work for the benefit of someone else. If you want to learn the power of being rich, you must turn these stereotypes upside down. You must be willing to go against the grain, and you must disrupt your conditioned thoughts.

The mind is the most remarkable, yet unexplored and inadequately understood power on earth. Each of us has the ability to accomplish whatever it is we set out to do.

There is nothing that's unattainable or unachievable that falls within your unique abilities. You may not have the unique ability to play shortstop for the New York Yankees, but your abilities may allow you to become the General Manager.

Another reason not to take extreme ownership is that it's much easier to conform. The reason we conform is because of what's referred to as the reptilian brain. Our mind is constantly in protective mode; fight or flight... keeping us from harm, or what we perceive as a threat, fear of danger.

For more than half of my life, my mind had it wrong. Resistance kept me from advancing further. My reptilian brain did everything in its power to keep me safe. It liked my house, my cars, my comforts. It liked my income right where it was. It also liked my struggles – not too much, but not too little—they were just right. It knew exactly how far to take things without going over the threshold of failure.

In taking extreme ownership, I had to get past this. I had to let go of the old ways of thinking. I had to constantly reinforce my goals, dreams, and desires one hundred percent of the time. I had to, as Earl Nightingale says, become what I think about all day long. I had to work at it again, and again and again. And if I found myself going back to old thoughts, old ways, I didn't beat myself up for it. I simply refocused and reset my new way of thinking. Eventually, procrastination and conformity became words of the past.

What you'll find when you take extreme ownership is that naturally you'll outwork everyone. You won't necessarily be working harder, or even smarter. You'll simply avoid wasting time on nonsense. Your mind will expand and your expectations will rise. You will no longer need to do what's familiar. You will transcend pettiness. Your expectations of yourself will soar and so will your results. No longer will your options be limited, they'll become limitless. You won't be pressured, forced, or drawn to what others might want you to do.

In fact, common sense will no longer be common. Sense will never look the same. Sense will have a whole new meaning. Your *sense* will vibrate at a higher frequency. You sense will look odd to others. Your *sense* will set you apart and your mind will be ready to accept the power of being rich.

"FAMILIARITY BREEDS CONTEMPT."

—Geoffrey Chaucer

Conformity

You've heard the old saying, "Familiarity breeds contempt." This is true with the vast majority of people, who get complacent and conform to what they're *supposed to do*, rather than living out what they are *destined* to do.

Most of my career, I conformed. Most of my career I worked hard for someone else. My true happiness was being sacrificed to my career. Don't get me wrong, I have been blessed to have been surrounded by countless good people. My wife and I and our friends had loads of fun. We dined out 3-4 times per week. We traveled. We enjoyed a very *comfortable* lifestyle and we have many wonderful memories. But today, I wish I had half of those days and nights back to invest in me.

Conformity is defined as an action in accordance with some specified standard. Standards may be useful tools, but if you're wanting to be rich, they're not a good model for living your life to the fullest. You may have standard rituals that you live by each day, but the goals you set for your life should not be in accordance with some specified standard.

Conformity acts like a chameleon, blending in with the rest. It's your job not to blend in and to identify conformity when it shows up.

- I'll wake up at 7:00 A.M. because that's the time most other people wake up.

- I'll watch the morning news because that's what most people do.
- I'll stop by McDonald's and order an Egg McMuffin because many other people do it too.
- I'll work from 9-5 because everyone else I work with does that too.
- I'll smoke because everyone else smokes.
- I'll drink alcohol because it's the thing to do.
- I'll relax every night, sit on the couch, and watch TV because that's what most people do.
- I'll fill up my weekends by going out at night, sleeping in late, and vegging out.
- I'm able to justify anything unproductive because everyone else does it exactly the same way.

Do you see the point? We conform. We justify. We become conditioned. We make excuses. We tell ourselves, "That's the norm." Many of our habits are formed from what we observed growing up, so therefore we *think* they're okay. If you truly want to become rich, you can no longer procrastinate, and you can no longer conform. You have to begin thinking differently. You have to take command, to take control. And as David Meltzer says, you have to "become a student of your calendar," optimizing your months, days, hours, minutes and seconds with precision.

The Proprietary Mind

For more than twenty years, my experience in the business world conditioned me for 'proprietary' thinking. What does this mean? Here are some examples:

I own this idea.

It's mine.

It's my intellectual capital and I'm not sharing it with anyone!

They can learn it on their own, the way I did!

I'm not going to make it easier for them.

Sharing information may put them on par with me.

The proprietary mind is a competitive mind. There is no competition unless we make it for ourselves. Again, try turning this concept upside down. You may think competitively about others because that's the way you were conditioned.

They are better looking.

They have more money.

They are in a happy relationship.

They have exceptional children.

The list can go on and on, yet this type of mindset doesn't bode well for prosperity. This type of mindset is smothered in judgment. This type of mindset closes off the neural pathways for sharing thoughts, ideas, and a general willingness to be helpful.

That's why it's so important to love what you do. It's important to find a career that fits your skill set so you have no worries sharing any kind of information. Often, people hold back information because they are not confident in themselves, or don't love what they do. Providing others with ideas, free information, free content and free collaboration — without expecting anything in return — is now the standard. If you are not being a good ambassador for your cause, someone else will.

Today, because of the Internet and all of the powerful tools and apps that we have at our disposal, there's nothing we can't solve. We are able to share and exchange so much good will through social media and all of the other tools available to us! Take advantage and don't get left behind.

I have no secrets and I have no proprietary insights that I'll hold back. Every resource, book, website, podcast, influencer, mentor, or tip that I have, you will receive. My expectation is that you choose to do the same for those you encounter. The more we can share as a society, the higher the frequency of goodness we will create.

Only GOOD things come from SHARING information. That's why Wikipedia, YouTube and Google are thriving. They have been able to give their biggest asset (knowledge and information) away for free and have found alternate ways to generate revenue. They didn't put the money first. They put sharing first.

In 2018, I had the privilege to interview neurosurgeon Dr. Khalid Sethi on my podcast. He offered many great pieces of advice during our conversation. One thing that stuck with me was this. He said that as a youngster, his grandfather offered him splendid counsel. He told him, "Don't chase the money... don't ever chase the money. If you love what you do and you don't chase the money, the money will chase you."

I love that phrase. Please adopt it.

Don't Play the role of Victim

One of the most critical components of personal fulfillment is never to play the victim. Even if you feel you're the victim, don't play it. Overcome it: renouncing victimhood is essential to awaken the power of being rich. There's no grey area.

Those who play victim are "never wrong."

Those who play victim are typically lazy.

Those who play victim look for handouts.

Those who play victim feel entitled.

Those who play victim can't meet deadlines.

Those who play victim make excuses.

Those who play victim don't have their eyes on the prize.

And those who play victim DO NOT TAKE EXTREME OWNERSHIP!

This old-school way-of-thinking is ancient history.

Resistance

Extreme ownership is not a cliché, it's the principle of a mindset, which you must be willing to live by every single day. The quicker you can come to that realization, the greater impact you will see for yourself, and for everyone you encounter.

Extreme ownership starts and ends with you. The impact it will have beyond you is tremendous, but that's not the reason to adopt the mindset. The reason to adopt it should be for you to set yourself up for success. Every encounter, every situation should and must be viewed from an extreme ownership mindset.

Your taking charge of extreme ownership will be contagious. Yes, THAT'S A WARNING! As you lead by example, assuming full accountability, responsibility, and ownership for your actions; others will follow suit and that's a very good thing. But not all of this will come without resistance.

Nothing good and nothing bad comes without resistance from the opposite perspective. That is the law of polarity. We will discuss the specific law in more detail in Chapter 7, but here is what the law states: for anything to exist, there has to be an equal and exact opposite. As an example, you cannot experience loss without experiencing some form of gain. In essence, the more good you do, the greater the resistance will be. I cannot emphasize this fact enough. Resistance is very real. You have to be on top of your game at every moment, so when you meet resistance you can greet it face on, and then gracefully push it away.

Chapter 4
Your Life Journey

Today,
I am rich!

The Journey

The power of being rich is a process, a lifelong journey. Your riches won't happen overnight. You likely won't wake up one day and say, "Today, I am rich!" But you will know when you come into richness. It's hard to word it, yet you will have a very special feeling inside. The feeling of being rich is like no other. It is ecstasy, joy, confidence, fullness, happiness, and love all in one. It is truly a power, The Power of Being Rich!

As in the other chapters, we note fundamental building blocks to each step in becoming rich. The life journey is an expression of it all – the obstacles and the overcoming. You cannot become rich, truly rich, without having a general understanding of where you are and where you want to go. You must have a destination, an aiming point of your target.

Take a step back and think about your last family trip on an airplane. For me it was taking our family to Florida for spring break. We flew from Philadelphia to Tampa. But what happened that day? When we boarded the plane did it miraculously get from Pennsylvania to Florida? If the window shades were closed it could certainly seem that way. But of course that's not the case. Planning and coordination were needed for my family and 120 other passengers to fly from Philadelphia to Tampa.

For starters, the mechanics had to complete a long checklist of items to ensure the plane was safe to fly. They had to add fuel. They had to load the luggage. The cleaning crew had to tidy the plane. It had to be restocked with food and refreshments. And now the hard part. The pilots had to plan the route. They had to use their skills and their brains to calculate the mission. Then, they had to put all of their training into practice to safely get the plane off the ground, follow their predetermined path, and then safely land the plane at the desired destination. If one form of resistance took them off course – a storm, another plane, or an irate passenger — the flight could end in disaster.

Our lives are like that flight, but most don't see it that way. If you have a dream, a goal, a destination — just like the plane — you must stay on course. You should have a vivid image of your aiming point in your mind's eye at all times. No matter what happens, you must stay on track. And, as with the plane, if you bump into a storm, you must go through it, or around it, but either way it's imperative to get back on course to reach your destination.

Wake Up to Your Reality

You have to wake up to the fact that in this life you are in full control. No one person or thing can control you. Become aware that each person has a desire to grow and prosper to the highest plateau they feel they can reach. But the reality is we all have different expectations of what prosperity means. Your desired plateau may be to impact a million people, whereas my desired plateau may be to impact only my family. Hence, we each have a different appreciation for what it means to be successful, or to be rich. But it's in our thoughts and dreams that we set our sights. The main objective is to have awareness. Be aware that you have the power to influence your desires. Be aware that you have the power to manifest outcomes. Be aware that you are now in full and complete control.

Many people are controlled by life instead of taking control of it. They fall under the influence of others, walking aimlessly along in their lives. You have to regain the power you once had before influence set in. You came into this world armed with every power and tool you needed to accomplish any desired goal. You now have to go back and regain the strength and knowledge, the *potential*, you had once possessed.

Setting Your Goals

If you can't think it, or dream it, you can't reach it. Setting goals will be a key requirement for walking a straight line through your life journey. But here's where you need, once again, to turn conditioned thinking upside down. Have the image of your goal in mind at all times, but don't get obsessive about it. Working towards your goal should be as natural as brushing your teeth or tying your shoes. It has to become a habit. Don't let your goal preoccupy your mind. Don't force your goal. Don't immerse or enwrap your thoughts into your goal. Let it be.

You are much better off paying strict attention to keeping negative energy and thoughts away while not foregrounding the importance of your goals. Wanting, longing, wishing, and needing create an energy counterproductive to obtaining the goal itself. This is where a mature mind rises above a naive mind. A mature mind knows longing creates feelings of anxiety, while a naive mind fails to learn and wastes energy in the non-act of mere yearning.

Fran Heath, my Little League baseball coach, taught me the meaning of trying too hard. I was a pitcher and I threw the ball quite hard for a nine-year-old. During warm-ups, I was able to throw a strike eight out of ten times. Yet, as soon as a batter came up to the plate I could no longer throw a strike. I would throw the ball in the dirt, I would throw the ball three feet over the batter's head, and I would throw the ball so far outside that the catcher couldn't reach it. Coach Heath worked with me week after week for the entire season. His technique was this. He told me to erase the batter from my mind. "Roger, the batter is not there, do you understand?" He reinforced that message every single pitch.

"The batter is not there!" he'd yell from the dugout – every single pitch. I made progress that first year, but it was painful. There were times I'd walk 4-5 hitters in a row. My mind was not mature enough to eliminate all other thoughts. I was focused on the batter, focused on what my teammates were thinking, focused on not wanting to embarrass my parents. Then, at some point the next year it clicked. I was able to shut everything else out and concentrate on the catcher's mitt. My target was that mitt. I would do everything in my power to hit that mitt exactly where it was.

By the time I was eleven, I threw my first no-hitter. By the time I was twelve I threw four no-hitters. Donny Stocks and I were the 1-2 and we were unstoppable. Throwing a strike became easy. Hitting the target wasn't even a question. Batter? I didn't even know who the kids were on the other team. That example taught me there's *no reason to try too hard*, ever.

The next phase of understanding a goal is that if you can think it and steadily work toward it without trying too hard, you will understand it's already there. In fact, anything you can think of is already there. It already exists because of your thoughts. Remember, your thoughts are energy – and the energy it took to imagine the thought made the thought itself real. It truly exists. Manifesting your reality is the realization that your goals are already achieved and therefore your desired reality already exists. If you take on that mindset it is gratifying and calming. Conversely, if you take on a longing mindset, or a mindset where you try too hard, it is stressful and worrisome.

Once you achieve this breakthrough, opportunity opens. No longer will you have to force opportunity, or stress over opportunity — opportunity will come to you. The key is not to think or worry about "how" you will achieve your goal. Leave that up to a much greater power. Trust that if you go about your day while keeping your goal in mind without obsessing or worrying about how you will achieve it, doors will start to open. When this happens, your uncertainty and fears will vanish. Trust the process, don't doubt the process. Embrace the process, and continue to keep your head down working toward your goal. When a door opens, smile and be grateful – thankful for its entry.

When setting your goals while moving through your life journey, a central rule is to expand your goals along the way. Don't hold the same goal day after day, week after week. It is our inherent purpose to expand our goals just as we expand our experience and knowledge. This is crucial in realizing the power of being rich. Our natural and instinctive desire is to continually expand, produce, create, and multiply more energy and life. Our goals are no different. If you keep choosing the same goals, your narrowed purpose will be contrary to the natural laws we live by. As with the farmer, your goal is not only to plant the seed, but to attain each increased level of growth along the way.

The Seed

Goal #1 – Plant the seed.

Goal # 2 – The seed is germinated.

Goal #3 – The seed produces its first roots and leaves, becoming a seedling.

Goal #4 – The seedling matures into a flowering plant.

Goal #5 – Pollination occurs and the flowers transform into fruit, containing seeds.

Your goals should work in the same way. Plant the seed of your goal in your mind with the intention to care for that seed and provide the necessary environment for your idea to grow into its next phase. Goals, as with seeds, are not achievable with the thought of the goal alone. It is perfectly natural to increase the size and number of goals and desires as you learn how to steadily achieve them.

Your initial vision is the impetus for setting any creative idea in motion. Holding that vision, having faith and trust in that vision, and taking positive action toward that vision will allow a chain of events to occur for your vision to materialize into matter. Rest assured that whatever your vision, it already exists and is already in motion and as you're pursuing it, it is pursuing you.

Think of it this way: pollination cannot occur without the transfer of pollen from an external force to the stamen of a plant. The patient plant relies on another force of energy for the transfer, be it wind, birds, or insects. Just how that happens, the plant doesn't care. As with the pollination process, how you reach your goals should not be directed or administered by you. Leave that process to a higher power.

MANIFESTING YOUR REALITY IS THE REALIZATION THAT YOUR GOALS ARE ALREADY ACHIEVED AND THEREFORE YOUR DESIRED REALITY ALREADY EXISTS.

You're the Star of Your Own Movie

Peter Sage was a guest on my podcast and we had an astonishing three-hour long conversation. Peter has a brilliant mind. Early on in his career he trained under Tony Robbins and he has extensive experience when it comes to personal growth and development. The biggest lesson I took away from my interview with Peter was an analogy he gave about being the star of your own movie.

Think of your life journey as a movie. Your movie has a script and it has a cast of characters. Do you want to play the lead role? Do you want to be the star? Or are you going to be a supporting actor or – worse yet – an extra? Peter's description of this is powerful, and I would do you a disservice if I didn't record it here for you to read. Here's what he said.

"Most people unfortunately are walking around as film extras in everybody else's movie because they don't own that power. They're complaining that the director and the producer of their movie hasn't given them the golden script. They get resentful because they think, 'Everybody else has a better movie than me.' That's victim mentality. That's the 'to me' mentality. Stop wishing about the fact that you've got to train and start focusing on the fact that you were born to get a medal. You are co-creating your script. Let's call it 'Life: the Movie.' Where were we before we came here? You can hypothesize that, but it was certainly non-physical. I like using the movie metaphor because people can relate to it. If we were to pick up a script, there's a difference between the character that you're playing in this movie, called Roger, and the actor that is playing that role, which is your consciousness. If you can, make a distinction between those two. Before you came here you were the actor and you picked up a script and it was for this particular computer game called Earth in the year 1969. Where did we come from before? Again, you can hypothesize, but don't get caught up about it – it's above our pay grade. I came here with a script. I believe I chose my parents. I think that's a powerful belief to have because there's an international epidemic called 'Let's blame our parents for everything.' And if I chose my parents, as dysfunctional as they were or weren't, what does that mean? Maybe I was here to learn something from them. Just because I didn't like the gym I was put into for the early workouts doesn't mean I didn't choose to become an athlete before I came here. So, I pick up the script, and now I have a particular predisposition to whatever my truth is and how that script goes, which is why we have a calling. It's why sometimes we feel drawn to things. It's why we have a passion to evolve into certain things, and it's why we feel resistance to things that are not in line with that. We each have an individual script that is a really good guideline on where we want to go. How we get there comes down to something called free will. As the star of the movie of my life, my job is to show up as the best I can be, listen to what is my intuition, and try to do the right thing. Place one foot in front of the other as best we can. Choosing love instead of fear in ever more challenging circumstances is the gateway to a happier life of growth and service. If we get to a point where we are going off track, we will get escalating feedback, from the director and the producer, or whatever label you want to call it that's designed to bring us on track. And if we don't listen to that? Well, there's a reason we call it escalating feedback."

Love Yourself

Self-love is the single most important topic in this book, and is certainly the single most important characteristic needed in order to claim the power of being rich. Without loving yourself, nothing else will be in sync. Just as it's not healthy to play the supporting role in someone else's movie, it's not healthy to look at others and think they have it better, or easier. Or, you want to be more like them and less like you. That's the same as looking in on someone's world and feeling they have a better script. We are here to love and to be loved, but neither process can happen at its full capacity unless you love yourself first.

Loving yourself means accepting your shortcomings.

Loving yourself means embracing your scars.

Loving yourself means being non-judgmental of your physical being.

Loving yourself means recognizing your uniqueness.

Loving yourself means focusing on your strengths.

Loving yourself means doing unto yourself as you do unto others.

Loving yourself means respecting yourself.

Loving yourself means not living up to someone else's standards.

Loving yourself means having high self-esteem.

Loving yourself means you are all-deserving.

Loving yourself means you're the star of your own movie.

Beyond a doubt, you have to love yourself first before others can love you in return. It's reciprocal. When you begin to put yourself first and take care of your mind, body, and spirit, then and only then will you see love around you thrive. Love will pour in from all sources.

People will be drawn to you because your internal love of yourself will shine upon others. The cause of self-love will produce the effect of others loving you, and it is infallible. It's like the law of gravity. When you toss a ball up in the air it will always come down, one hundred percent of the time, just as when you love yourself, others will love you in return.

Faith

Faith is not something you can force. Faith is not something you can fake. The only way to have faith is having faith in yourself. Trust that the hard work you put into each day has exponential payoff. Trust the coincidences that occur. Trust that they are in reality a direct correlation to your effort. Every action has an equal and opposite reaction. You cannot have true faith without seeing true results. And you will not see results without having faith. A result is a by-product of faith. And when doubt creeps in, let it go. Bring yourself back to center and reset. Just as with your goal, you cannot obsess over faith. Faith is just that… faith. Don't overthink it. Don't overplay it. Don't obsess over it. All you have to do is believe.

Failure

A big part of the life journey is failure. We cannot progress or learn without failing. Failure is a gift. Failure is a lesson. Failure is a necessary component of success. Without failure, we cannot advance.

Every great leader will tell you they are where they are because of failure. They were able to rise to the next occasion because they were knocked down. They were able to succeed in life because they overcame failure. Embrace your failures. Accept each one of them as a stepping stone to your ultimate goal and fulfillment of being rich.

It is, however, up to each one of us to take the actions and learnings of failure and put them into motion. It doesn't take a toddler long to figure out not to touch a hot stove. Hot means hot and if they touch the stove again it would be a failure in the form of a burn. We hear the expression "Live and Learn," but there's a big piece of the puzzle that's missing. What about "Live, Learn and Grow"? If we do not grow from our failures we will stay complacent. Growth and prosperity are instinctive traits of human life. Unfortunately, society often gets in the way and a vast majority of people conform. Recognize this as your opportunity to differ. Recognize this as a distinct advantage in your pursuit of being rich.

The Rumble Strip

Peter Sage told me his rumble strip analogy and it's another gem I'd like to share.

"Our life journey," he said, "is like the rumble strip on the freeway. You're driving down and there's a rumble strip on each side that's designed to keep you on track—thankfully. Now I use a health metaphor. I'm going along the freeway of life and I'm listening to my music, and

I'm chomping my Doritos, Big Mac, and going to drive-throughs. And all of a sudden, I hit the rumble strip. I see that I start getting out of breath walking up stairs for the first time, and I'm not happy with it. What do most people do? Well, that rumble strip is interfering with my music so they turn up the music. And then guess what happens? If you're lucky you may get a mild heart attack. Or, you may have a stroke. Or, it may be you just didn't listen to the rumble strip and you go off the edge and you don't come back. Turn down the music, pay attention and take different action."

I'm sure you can relate to the rumble strip analogy. We all can. The key question is: are we listening? We know when we're getting off track. We know when we hit the bumps. They're obvious and they're jolting. Are you going to continue to mask them? Are you going to continue to pretend they're not there? Or, are you going to jerk the steering wheel back on track and listen to your inner voice? We are all born with these incredible instinctive gifts. It took millions of years for us to get here. Be appreciative of them. Be grateful for your instincts. Stop keeping all of your marvelous gems locked up. You have the key. Unlock your gems and start acknowledging your greatness.

Confidence

This is where you'll hopefully begin to see and realize the pattern. To have confidence, relinquish the desire to be confident. Put less importance on being confident. When you put importance on confidence, that's called an insecurity. When you put less importance on anything, your power to become rich will increase. That's why it's easy to distinguish a confident person from an arrogant one. Arrogant people are putting emphasis on the need to be confident. Confident people put an emphasis on their own beliefs. Confident people do not need to pretend, or abuse, or overcompensate. Confident people can rely on being their true and authentic self.

Confidence is attractive.

Arrogance is repulsive.

Confidence is beautiful.

Arrogance is ugly.

Confidence doesn't require justification.

Arrogance begs for acceptance.

"Turn down the music, pay attention and take different action."

—Peter Sage

Chapter 5
The Paradox: You're Already Rich

When your intention is to manifest what you already have, it becomes easier and easier to achieve.

You're already rich

You were born rich. You were born with all of the tools, gifts, knowledge and understanding needed to obtain your riches. What's ironic is that a vast majority of people are searching everywhere for their riches, failing to look in the most obvious place. They fail to look within.

Rich people take comfort looking within. Rich people enjoy being alone. Rich people do not get bored. Rich people make the most of each day because they are aware that life is an evolution and an ever growing process.

The paradox is that most do not recognize what they already have. People are too busy obsessing over what they don't have, or what someone else has, and are blind to the fact that if they took the time to put in their reps [?], they would surely start to see some results.

Intentional Desire

How do you begin to embrace the paradox if you don't yet understand the paradox? As with each chapter in this book, all of these principles arise and appear by way of intention and practice. You can't just say you're rich and *voilà!* you become rich. It is a matter of repeating, while truly believing in, your desired intention.

When your intention is to manifest what you already have, it becomes easier and easier to achieve. The disconnect most people have is that they don't TRULY believe they can achieve their desired outcome.

If you truly believe, in your heart, that your desired outcome is real, it will become emphatically real. But if you have the slightest amount of doubt, that doubt will overtake your intentions.

When you intend something, it is paramount to stake your claim. Be proud of it. Speak it. Declare it yours. See it clearly in your thoughts. If you can think it, you can claim it. Thoughts are vibrations of energy and once you create the thought the intention of claiming that thought already exists.

Don't be shy about giving yourself a pep talk about what it is you desire. It's perfectly okay to have a productive conversation with yourself. The repetition of intention is as important as the intention itself. By speaking the intention you take the intention to a higher level. It is no longer just a thought. It is a thought that has been put into action.

Affirmations are a powerful tool to set in motion your desires. I will disclose to you my list of daily affirmations in due time. But first, think about yours. What intentions do you have? What desires do you cherish? Write them down. Repeat them to yourself. Speak them aloud so they can vibrate at a higher level of energy. Believe them with all of your will.

Finding Your Unique and Authentic Voice

Now that you have voiced your desire to obtain the riches that you already have, it's time to express your inner soul to the outside world. This is living your true passion and purpose. This is expressing your truth. This is your calling. This is finding your unique and authentic voice and truly being yourself.

Being yourself will open doors.

Being yourself is being of service.

Being yourself keeps you present.

Being yourself provides full transparency.

Being yourself makes you a better listener.

Being yourself provides endless opportunities.

Being yourself dismisses conflicting internal intentions.

Being yourself allows you to manifest anything you desire.

"BE MORE INTERESTED THAN INTERESTING."

—David Meltzer

Finding your true and authentic voice will allow you to set the world on fire. You will be able to speak at ease and people will be drawn to your authenticity; as authenticity cannot be manipulated. Each of us has a unique ability to read others' authenticity, knowing whether it is there, or not.

When you find your authentic voice, match it with outer intention: there is nothing that cannot be realized, including that you're already rich. Manifesting outcomes will become a habitual way of thinking.

Embrace Your Unique Abilities

About a decade ago, a friend of mine turned me on to an assessment test called the Kolbe Index, established by Kathy Kolbe. The results of a Kolbe assessment are geared toward helping you identify your unique abilities. There are four major categories measured and scored in the assessment.

- Fact Finder

- Follow Through

- Quick Start

- Implementor

Once complete, you receive your "Kolbe Score" along with an assessment. My Kolbe score is 2883 and the following is a transcript of my assessment.

"You are intuitive... you are highly intuitive and you intuit things before they happen and because you see the trend, you see the pattern and you see how it's going to play out. So when you say to somebody, 'watch out... this is likely to happen if you keep doing that,' they're going to think you have a crystal ball. What you have is an uncanny instinct for predicting the future because you integrate what's happening into a system that takes you into that visionary quick-start future. This is not a spooky thing, this is a very measurable, quantifiable talent. Don't be afraid of it — enjoy it, relish it. Don't try to explain it to other people because they may not get it, but don't deny it, don't demean it — trust it and you're going to do amazing things with it."

Since taking that test, I have aimed to capitalize on my strengths and embrace my weaknesses, not only in the sense of admitting them, but seeking out help in areas where I am weak, such as in fact-finding and implementation. Becoming aware of my strengths and weaknesses helped me to rise above knowing who I am inside and out.

As with the paradox discussed in this chapter, the Kolbe assessment only reinforced what I already knew. I knew I'm highly intuitive. I knew I have an uncanny instinct for predicting the future. I say this just as you know your unique abilities. You don't need to take the Kolbe assessment unless you're looking to justify what you already know. You see, you need to give yourself more credit for what you do know rather than beating yourself up for what you don't know.

Vulnerability

For my entire life, I was taught to stand clear of being vulnerable. To a person growing up, and growing into the business world, vulnerability meant weakness. Showing you are vulnerable meant you are susceptible, powerless, defenseless and helpless.

During my quest to realize the power of being rich, I found that vulnerability had an entirely new meaning. In fact, vulnerability became a necessity and in some ways my best friend. I say this because when you let yourself become vulnerable magic takes place. Our instincts can sense when we're being vulnerable. When this happens, our guard comes down. When this happens people are more susceptible to reaching out. When this happens your transparency will reflect back to others like a reflection in a mirror.

Vulnerability is being real.

Vulnerability is pureness.

Vulnerability is innocence.

Vulnerability is confidence.

Vulnerability is remaining open.

Vulnerability is deepness.

Vulnerability is creativity.

Vulnerability is maturation.

Vulnerability is the **TRUE YOU!**

Trust

For many, having trust in yourself is often the most complex quality of all. To trust is to have self-belief in your abilities, instincts, and skills without overcompensation. If you trust in yourself and have good intentions, your self-belief is always right and no one can argue otherwise.

Your unique characteristics – those that are the real you-ness of you – are your personal thumbprint. All of your past experience, all of your education, all of your victories and tragedies add up to who you are. Embrace your life learnings, put them into practice, and feel comfortable in your own skin.

Fully embracing self-trust means you have a complete understanding that resides within your essential self and generates your own decision-making. It doesn't mean that you can't and won't make a mistake – that would be arrogance. It also means you will not be right 100% of the time in your decisions. In fact, we make hundreds, if not thousands of decisions per day, so do not put the pressure on yourself to be right every time.

Think about this... the best quarterbacks of all time have converted just 5-7% of plays to touchdowns when in the redone. The top ten hitters in Major League Baseball history have a batting average between .342 and .366. That includes names like Babe Ruth (.342), Ted Williams (.344), and Ty Cobb (.366).

So if your decision making is right even 50% of the time, you are a true winner.

Trusting in yourself and having conviction in your belief system is paramount to Finding Your Unique and Authentic Voice.

Live life like a lucid dream

Have you ever had a lucid dream? You know, the dream where you're aware that you're dreaming and you're able to take control within the dream. For me, it's a recurring dream. I'm a kid playing outside in front of our house and I suddenly realize I'm dreaming and then take control. I do what I've always wanted to do... I fly. I raise myself up and fly up and down our street, over the telephone wires, with full control of flight. Then, I venture off into the city, above the parks and buildings and railroad tracks... places I know. It is the best feeling in the world. I am free and I am in complete control.

What if this became your reality? What if you could control your life as you do in a lucid dream? I have some good news. You can.

Most of us fear we don't have the power to control our reality, when in fact we do. And most people avoid even trying to control their own reality. We tend to let life happen to us instead of controlling it as we do in a lucid dream. There were moments in your dream when you confronted obstacles that you mastered by re-conceiving them—nothing stood in your way. The trick is to live your life like this every single day.

If you take a step back and look at life as in a lucid dream where you control each move you make, you can start to see the movie script Peter Sage described, where each person you encounter is playing a role in your movie.

They will interact with you in different ways, some obstructing, some assisting. The key factor is for you to observe the movie from a distance so you can understand it and realize the paradox that already exists.

"Gratitude opens the door to abundance consciousness."

—Deepak Chopra

Everything discussed thus far has been focused on the self – self love, trust, failure, goals, resistance, awareness, optimism, attitude, non-judgement, vulnerability, setting goals, conformity, and intentional desire. It is now crucial that you observe these principles and apply them to be in unison with a higher source, a higher power that you may call God, the Universe, or the Higher Source. For ease of reference, I will call the higher source God.

When you convey your thoughts and desires, and shape them into wants and needs, you are conveying them to God. God is the energy force that directs and produces in ways we cannot and should not question. God will take care of the how.

Pretend you have a thought to write the music to be performed by a symphony orchestra. You have a complete grasp of the entire performance and know how you want it to show up in the world. Your thoughts are transferred to paper and the music starts to form. These are your goals. You have written them, you have spoken them, and you have practiced them. Your idea has come to life. But you cannot carry out the performance by yourself. There are many elements that need to come together for the music to be played. Your idea has been set in motion and you continue to work toward that idea to help the symphony come to life. The first thing you do is secure the best conductor because without him your masterpiece will not be in tune. Then, you recruit the musicians for each instrument, you secure the venue to perform, you market the show for the grand opening, and you are all set to go. You have multiple rehearsals and you thank the musicians for all of their effort, but you fail to thank the conductor. Night after night you forget to thank him. On opening night, you sit in the front row dead center, surrounded by all of your loved ones. Then, just before the symphony begins, you receive a text message from the conductor that he took another job. He's moved to Boston and he won't be there to direct your orchestra. The show begins, but there's no conductor. The music is playing, but it's not in sync. Your orchestra is missing the most important piece. You try to jump in last minute to help, but it's no use. You're not properly trained and the performance turns out to be a debacle.

You can have the best ideas and intentions in the world and you may get lucky here and there. But in order for your thoughts and ideas to be in harmony with your outcomes, you must act in a specific way to be in absolute balance with God. Your creativity, ideas, wants, and ultimate richness cannot be sustained without the inclusion and practice of gratitude. And everything mentioned in this book cannot be sustained without the inclusion and practice of gratitude. If you had shown the composer some gratitude, the outcome would have likely been different.

Deepak Chopra says, "Gratitude opens the door to abundance consciousness," meaning without gratitude, you can never truly realize abundance. And in order to realize abundance you have to act in a specific way. Gratitude is the fuel that propels your creativity to your desired outcome. It is a source of energy needed to elevate your higher self.

So what does this all mean? If you truly believe and have faith in God and in the process of how all things work, you can leave the *how* up to God. Not only is it the right thing to do, it also takes tremendous pressure off of your mind. When you leave the *how*, the hardest part of the process to God, your abundance and riches are endless. No longer will you worry. No longer will you fear. Your mind can focus on what it is intended to do and that's create and grow in unison with everything else in the world that is also acting in a specific way. You will begin to look at things differently. No longer will you look at a healthy plant as an object. That plant is growing just as you are growing. That plant is leaving the *how* to God. Now, the plant will rely on certain things to be healthy, just as you will rely on certain things. The plant needs good soil and water and sunlight. If it does not have those things it will not thrive and may not even survive. Yet do your part, act in a specific way, and practice daily gratitude, and God will return everything you desire.

Other people you observe may have extreme wealth — the biggest house, the most extravagant cars – and may travel the world, wear the most expensive clothes and jewelry, eat and drink at the finest restaurants — but what if they're missing one piece? Just as with the symphony, what if they're not in communication with the conductor?

If they're not, they will never experience the true power of being rich. Life cannot and will not be in true harmony. That law, like all other universal laws, is inflexible. You may observe that someone else "has it all" but one doesn't know if another has true riches. True wealth consists in experiencing all of life's abundance plus having abundance in your relationship with God.

Gratitude is an expression of your appreciation from your physical being, through your spiritual being, to arrive at its final destination, the higher source, God. When you express gratitude, just as when you pray, the energy you create is an expression of your soul.

Start by asking yourself, "What am I grateful for?" It's a powerful exercise. When you take the time to truly think about everything you're grateful for, your awareness will trigger a tremendous amount of positive energy.

You can use every tool listed in this book, as well as every other tool ever provided, to help guide you on your path in realizing the power of being rich. However, it is essential to have a clear and distinct feeling of gratitude in and for all that you do. If you don't, you will never experience true richness.

The idea is to keep the momentum of creative thoughts moving toward you, realizing that in order to make this happen it is necessary to contemplate, to activate, your thoughts, wants and desires in the form of gratitude. Send your thoughts out and encapsulate them as gratitude and they will return abundance.

Think of it this way. Imagine you pull up to the drive-thru of a bank and you have access to an account in your name with unlimited funds. You pick up the container, write out a withdrawal form, sign it and send it on its way. As you're waiting, you have thoughts of gratitude for the unlimited funds you have, knowing you are doing good work and making a difference in the world. You are thankful for all that you have. Within a matter of minutes, the container comes back to you with exactly what you requested on the form. The currency may come back slightly different than you intended, but the amount of the currency is an exact match to what you ordered.

The law of gratitude works the same way because you already have access to abundance. You already possess all of the tools to access your riches. You already have the skills and knowledge to access whatever it is you truly desire. The problem is, you didn't show your gratitude to the conductor and the conductor failed to show. It's time to practice gratitude.

Gratitude is being thankful.
Gratitude is being appreciative.
Gratitude is being grateful.
Gratitude is returned kindness.
Gratitude is an acknowledgment of goodness.
Gratitude is a practice and skill.
Gratitude delivers boundless returns.

The Rule of Gratitude

The purpose of gratitude is to develop an "attitude of gratitude" toward everything that has come to you previously, everything that comes to you in the present, and everything that is yet to come your way. You must be willing to accept gratitude as a rule.

While it is necessary to live and stay in the present, it is purposeful to be grateful for all things granted to you at any point in time. The practice of this will become habit-forming, so there's no longer a conscious thought of needing to practice gratitude. The practice will become as natural as needing to eat. It will become part of you.

What if you don't know where to begin? Try practicing gratitude twice daily — practicing gratitude the moment you wake, and right before you go to sleep. If you follow this practice, you will be certain to find success in adopting the rule.

Gradually, the practice of gratitude will grow with you as part of acting in a specific way. This consistency of the action of gratitude will deliver your desires just as rapidly in return. When you open your heart to gratitude, there is no bigger joy in the world.

Competitive Thinking

Competitive thinking is the mind's way of justifying a lack of fulfillment which you feel because in essence you have a lack of gratitude. When there's a lack of gratitude, it's easy for the mind to wander and focus on negative and judgmental thoughts. These thoughts spur feelings of envy and fear. When you focus your thoughts on gratitude and stay in your own lane, you will avoid hitting the rumble strip on either side of the road. Those that tend to focus their thoughts on inferiority, doubt, poverty, lack, and misfortune will also get these things in return. They have hit the rumble strip, and find it harder and harder to get back on the freeway. The cars that are zipping past them are those that are focused on their goals, not worrying about what others have, or what they don't have. It is a slippery slope and if you do hit the rumble strip, you must get back on the freeway just as soon as you possibly can.

Can I get a thank you?

How often are you practicing thank you? A thank you in the physical world is the equivalent to expressing gratitude to a higher source. When you express thanks in a genuine way, it too becomes a powerful source of energy. When you thank another person, you demonstrate your sincerity in that expression. When you take things for granted, failing to make a conscious effort in providing an expression of thanks, that too can take your symphony out of harmony.

Each day we have ample opportunity to express our thanks and gratitude. They're two small words that keep life in harmony. Say the words often. Make it part of your practice of acting in a specific way.

"The gratitude challenge requires simply saying 'thank you' when you wake up and when you go to sleep; contemplating the many things in your life that you are thankful for."

—David Meltzer

Forgiveness & Empathy

"Forgiveness allows you to connect with your soul," says Deepak Chopra. Letting go of resentment, hostility, and judgment is a two-way street and is one more principle that lets you realize the power of being rich. When you are rich, you are able to both forgive and ask for forgiveness — no matter how sinister the act. You cannot fulfill the completion of richness without having a full acceptance of forgiveness.

Forgiveness does not seek retribution.

Forgiveness does not look for punishment.

Forgiveness does not judge.

Forgiveness does not hold another hostage.

Forgiveness does not beg for penalty.

Forgiveness does not want ill-will.

Forgiveness does not encourage payback.

Forgiveness does not ask for revenge.

Forgiveness is the sign of a mature heart and mind. Anything opposite to forgiveness falls in line with negativity. Your mind will be preoccupied with negative thoughts of the act and will reverberate with the things you don't like about the person or persons in dispute. Remember, your thoughts and images will be returned to you whether they are positive or negative. Thoughts about things you don't like will work against the things you do like. The act of forgiveness, or lack of forgiveness, accelerates the desire. Arm yourself with all of the tools to return to you what is good.

Empathy is the action of understanding, being aware of, being sensitive to, and vicariously experiencing the feelings, thoughts, and experience of another. The empathy can be either past- or present-directed, explicit or implied.

Having empathy is having an imaginative understanding, and you can practice it by being considerate of others' feelings. Too often this characteristic is underplayed in life. No one person fully understands what another person may be experiencing; therefore, no one person should ever be insensitive in an explicit manner. It is not our place to do so.

Do not equate empathy with either sympathy or compassion. Sympathy implies being able to share in the feelings of another — being sympathetic to them – while empathy is being able to imagine the feelings that one may not actually have. Compassion is having the ability to grasp someone's particular form of pain, and having a desire to alleviate that pain. All of these traits are good in the sense that they show an underlying hunger for goodness, yet empathy is the only one fulfilled by continual ongoing action.

"When you actually deploy attitude and empathy, you become numb to negativity which leads to pure offense, and speed, which leads to results."

—Gary Vaynerchuk

Chapter 7
The Laws of the Universe

"As you study and grow, your awareness deepens and so does your understanding."

—David Neagle

Universal law

There is not enough room in this book to do anything like justice to the laws of the universe, a vast topic. In fact, you should view this as only a brief introduction to universal law. The exciting news, though, is that when you start studying and practicing universal law, you'll see immediate results. Everything currently present in my life is the result of deliberate intention backed up my current understanding and practice of universal law. One key element I will communicate upfront: it's paramount not to brag or boast about the effect of universal law. I will expand on the concept in a while, but first let's tackle the need to reduce the importance or emphasis we place on things.

Too often, people get overly excited when they receive a gift from a higher source. Their inexperience and immaturity when receiving a gift or gifts can be overshadowed by placing too much importance on the gift and not following through on all of the principles that created the energy for that gift to be received. A mature mind realizes that placing importance on things only leads to disorder. When importance is placed on anything, it is a contrived assessment of its real form. Hence, when there is an elaborate emphasis on the importance of things, either positive or negative, there will be unbalance. This principle holds true for both inner and outer importance. Reduce importance the same way you might think about lowering your ego. No one wants to be with a bragger, just as no one wants to be in the company of arrogance.

There are many sources out there that provide a deep understanding of the laws of the universe. My number one priority has been to become a student of the laws, not only reading and learning about their meanings, but actually putting them into practice as part of a daily routine.

David Neagle has been my primary source of information when it comes to universal law. I read all that he writes and watch and listen to all of his content. David has over 30 years of experience with the laws of the universe and that experience is priceless.

David once wrote, "Many people over the years have asked me for a "cheat sheet" of Universal Laws, but the problem is that without studying them deeply and allowing for your own self-reflection, they are nothing more than words on paper."

I took those words to heart.

I study the laws of the universe deeply.

I embrace every chance to learn and grow in strength and knowledge of universal law.

The Law of Attraction

Whether or not you have studied the universal laws, there are some that you likely are already familiar with. For example, its certain you've heard of the law of attraction. Much of what has been discussed in this book can fall under the universal law of attraction. You will attract to yourself what you put out to the universe in the form of thoughts, voice, or action. Optimism attracts optimism. Pessimism attracts pessimism. You've heard that misery loves company, just as joy loves the same. When you are shaping your own destiny and manifesting your desires, you have every right to claim them as yours and to start doing so this very moment. No one can dictate your timetable for initiating your own law of attraction. It is yours for the taking.

When considering the law of attraction, simply make an effort to maintain a higher frequency. Be in tune with your higher self. Act on the many things discussed in this book – love, optimism, empathy, joy, productivity, advancement, creativity, growth, success and gratitude.

Attract into your life what you want to believe and receive.

The Law of Cause and Effect

This law has similarities to the law of attraction, but it is more closely related to Sir Isaac Newton's scientific law of motion: for every action, there's an equal and opposite reaction. This law, as with all laws, is inflexible. Whether you are aware of it or not, your life can be greatly impacted by the law of cause and effect. For example, throughout the day, your expressions of positive and negative impulse will return such actions to you. This interchange can impact relationships, as well as your physical environment. If you are wanting change, you must be the change first. If your desire is to advance in all that you do, you must begin by setting your actions at a higher frequency.

The Law of Polarity

The law of polarity states that for anything to exist, there has to be an equal and exact opposite. Anytime there is trouble, you can expect a reaction of goodness. For every death, there is birth, For every loss, there is gain. For every setback, there is progress. What we don't know, and should not judge, is when or how the law presents itself.

Understanding the law of polarity brings clarity to the reality of life. If you are in the field of sales, you understand this law well. For as long as you are working toward your goal with good intentions, you will surely find success. For every "no" there will be a "yes," but the receiving of a "yes" will be a complex variable in relation to the "no." For example, the success of the "yes" may take the effort of ten "no's." It is up to you to leave that formula to a much higher power. Just know, it is your job to continually work toward the "yes" and it will be fulfilled if you act in a specific way and with good intent.

The Law of Compensation

This law is perhaps the most important law when it comes to the power of being rich. The law simply states that you will reap what you sow. In other words, you can be compensated in many forms, including money, but how you live your life and treat others will determine your rewards. Even a wealthy person could end up a derelict if he or she doesn't care about the world around them.

The quality of the thought or effort you expend toward something will come back to you like a boomerang. What happens when you express extreme dislike or disgust for something? Your thoughts immediately go to a place of darkness. This can diminish or replace all of the good work you have done. The boomerang will return to you what your emotions sent out to the universe. Hold your emotions in check. Don't be reactive, rather be proactive and disciplined in all that you do.

Being of service

One of the sure ways to incorporate the laws of the universe into your life is to lead your life by serving others. When your mind is focused on being of service, its first intent is to give. Giving opens up the door to endless possibility. Giving comes in many shapes and forms – volunteer work, donations, helping support those in need, performing good deeds, or gifting to charitable causes. Being of service, or giving, is a crucial component in realizing the power of being rich.

Being of service stimulates kindness.

Being of service shows recognition to others.

Being of service opens your heart.

Being of service creates positive energy.

Being of service mobilizes cause and effect.

"FOR IT IS IN GIVING THAT WE RECEIVE."

—Saint Francis of Assisi

Chapter 8
Taking Extreme Action

"Momentum can take things that are average and make them extraordinary."

—Ed Mylett

Nothing can materialize without the intentional force of action. Action is the single most important principle in realizing your own power of being rich. You cannot be rich without action. Action is the difference between those who talk of being rich and those who take the steps that will ensure their richness.

Early on, we covered the ill effects of procrastination, conformity, and complacency. "Extreme action" means *nothing but action.* The trick is to act and act now, without hesitation and without questioning your instincts. If you hesitate, or wait, or procrastinate you will own that non-action, and that non-action in itself has a negative effect. Only those who take action can truly build momentum, realizing that progress is the result of the momentum built. One of the biggest principles in taking action is to lessen the importance of what will *come* from the action, or what people will *think* of the action. Perform the action as a deliberate intention. Perform the action without giving thought to the reaction.

Having a "do it now" mentality propels your energy in such a way to take immediate and extreme action. Whatever it is you desire, or hold in your mind's eye, take action on that thought immediately.

Perfection

Perfection is overrated and unattainable. When setting yourself up for success, it's imperative to lower the importance and even release the mindset of perfection. No one, or nothing is perfect just as no one and nothing is imperfect. As soon as you realize that all life is advancing, you will never again look at something as being perfect or imperfect. It is always in a constant state of increase. That means, remove yourself from the judgment of perfection.

My personal technique for this was to redefine perfection. For starters, when you lessen the importance of all things, it's easy to take more action. Each action you take should be a continual advancement of your personal growth. If each of us were tasked with building a "Yellow Brick Road" to our life of riches, think of each task you do, each action you take, as laying one brick in the road. The goal is to build a strong and stable road in order to reach the "Land of Oz," your life of riches. Are you going to hesitate in laying each brick? Are you going to ponder if each brick is exactly in line? Are you going to procrastinate in laying down your bricks, telling yourself you'll get to it in due time? Of course not. You wouldn't be able to lay the bricks fast enough. Wrap your mind around that concept. Understand the reasoning and urgency to take action in laying each brick down without 100% perfection. As soon as you can do this, you'll be in a position to take extreme action while looking through a different lens. In fact, your vision through your new lens will appear as if you're looking through a kaleidoscope. Unprecedented colors, shapes, thoughts, ideas, and forms will be seen. You will surely find ways to turn the eyepiece of your kaleidoscope in such a way as to see the beauty of everything before you. Objects will be accented with light. Everything you encounter will take on a new form because you are concentrating on the path to your goal, but not the importance of your goal.

As you begin to take action, lessen your feelings of desire and deepen your feelings of your purpose. You should be taking action toward your goal with ease of thought. It should be as easy as pouring a cup of coffee, and the only thing that can hamper it is letting fear enter your mind, or trying too hard to achieve perfection. Have your goal in your mind's eye, with your new kaleidoscope lens, and take action without obsession.

Momentum

Ed Mylett says, "Momentum can take things that are average and make them extraordinary." This is a continuation of the kaleidoscope example. When you take action and build momentum magic happens. You will see magic in average because with momentum you know you can make average extraordinary.

All life is energy, and that energy is either growing or waning, living or dying. Momentum gives your action increased energy. When you do things thoughtfully but swiftly, you gain momentum. When you do things thoughtfully but lack urgency, you lose momentum. An action-focused mind will come to expect action-focused intention. As you practice taking action, your mind will embrace it and provide immediate space for your next action. Your "Yellow Brick Road" to your "Land of Oz" will be complete sooner than you'd expect.

"SOMEONE TOLD ME ONCE TO LOOK DOWN AT YOUR FEET; THAT'S WHERE YOU'RE SUPPOSED TO BE."

–DAVID SCHUMANN

You are where you are because that's where you're supposed to be. David Schumann was a guest on my podcast. He made a statement a couple of years back that stuck with me. He said, "Someone told me once to look down at your feet; that's where you're supposed to be." His statement added momentum to my actions. That statement makes it valid to do things exactly where you are at the moment, physically and mentally, to do everything you can to take extreme action where you are. Do not wait for *when you get there* or *when you get around to it*. Do things where you are at each moment to carry your momentum through.

There are those who do the bare minimum to fill their space, or fill the hours in a day. Those who conform or procrastinate do not fill their current space. Taking extreme action is not only filling your current space, but it is *fulfilling* or even *transcending* your current space. Your momentum will provide for an even greater capacity to do more, be more, accomplish more, fit more, acquire more, accept more, and give more.

The sole purpose of life is to generate more life. The world has not advanced by procrastination. The world has advanced by extreme action. The same is true for you. You cannot advance as a person, you cannot advance your thoughts, you cannot advance in anything you do without taking action. If you are acting where you are, because that's where you're supposed to be, and if you are acting with earnest intention and with extreme action, you will only advance. And once you understand how the laws of the universe work in conjunction with your intended actions, there is no way you will fail. If you take positive action toward your goals; day after day, you will most certainly succeed in becoming rich.

Connect the Dots

When you were a child, you likely had a coloring book at home or in school called dot-to-dot. The object of a dot-to-dot drawing is to connect all of the dots so that they form a picture. If you follow the instructions for the intended path, the picture will come to life 100% of the time. If you do a quick Google search, you'll see that there are also dot-to-dot drawing books for adults. They are extreme and complex puzzles, bringing incredible scenes to life through an intense dot-to-dot process. It may take hours to complete one of these complex puzzles; however, the end result delivers an amazing image. When you initially look at the complex puzzle, the thought of completing it seems daunting. But as long as you stay the course, and connect the dots as they are intended, it will appear exactly as it was intended.

The same is true when you pursue your goals. Each action is equivalent to connecting one dot to the other. As long as you are working steadily toward your goal and acting in a specific way, you will most certainly reach your desired goal. You could not have predicted that connecting one dot to another would lead you there on that exact path, but when you look back at how you connected the dots, it makes clear, complete sense. Remember, it's imperative not to give thought or importance to the *how*.

Stay intent on taking swift and extreme action, but also respect your workload. Do not take on more than you can rightfully accomplish in a single day. You should give yourself ample time to complete your tasks so as not to rush or compromise them by moving too quickly. There must be a balance of thoughtful action, so that when you lay each brick on your path, it goes down not sloppily and carelessly, but with precision and ease. Overload can also be detrimental to your momentum, just as procrastination can stall your momentum. Be courteous to yourself and do today what you can do well, leaving tomorrow's work for tomorrow.

As when looking through a kaleidoscope, the colors of life will bring you tremendous positive energy. Your actions will be full of joy. Action will rouse enthusiasm. Your actions will bring a skip to your step; your intensity will become infectious. Your actions will raise the bar of those around you. Your actions will cause a ripple effect of momentum, from yourself and from others. Your actions will dictate that you are on a mission… a mission of service, and goodness, powered by belief in your desires and ultimate riches. Your actions will become your new identity.

"IN A GENTLE WAY, YOU CAN SHAKE THE WORLD."

—Mahatma Gandhi

Chapter 9
Your Right to Abundance

There is abundance for everyone because there is infinite abundance.

Contrary to what you may have been told, or heard, we do not live in a world of lack. If you believe that, you will certainly not realize the power of being rich. There is not one successful person on earth that believes we live in a world of lack. If they did, their success would no longer advance. We live in a world of abundance. There is enough abundance to go around for the 7+ billion people on this earth ten times over. Yet, our news reports, churches, social media and Internet would have you believing differently. Your abundance is rightfully yours and it's yours for the taking.

Did you ever stop to think about why rich people tend to stay rich and poor people tend to stay poor? It is the result of two things; mindset and will. If you are poor and have the mindset and desire to change your environment, and you begin conceiving, believing and working toward your goal of changing your environment, you will most certainly change it. If you are wealthy and have the mindset that you will continue to grow and expand and not be complacent, you will certainly continue to advance your wealth.

By now, you should have grasp firmly the importance of acting in a specific way in order to allow your energy, vibration, and frequency to be in tune with the greatest source of energy of all. When you are able to alleviate fear, doubt, worry, concern and to an extent, hope — that is when you most certainly will thrive and then come to the realization that you have every right to any form of abundance that exists. This realization acts like a light switch. Once you truly understand its principle and have faith and trust in the laws that support the principle, the light will remain in the "on" position. There is no turning it off, unless you divagate in your thoughts and beliefs.

Once you access this source and continue to act in a specific way, the floodgates will be open to you. Your new realization is that anything is possible and that there's a bountiful supply of anything you desire. Too often people have the mindset that there's not enough to go around. There's not enough money, there's not enough supply, there's not enough abundance. That very mindset goes against the universal laws. There is abundance for everyone because there is infinite abundance. Knowing you can rightfully manifest your outcomes as long as you act in a specific way, you find nothing that is out of reach. That is how the iPhone, Tesla, Boeing 777, and the Space Shuttle Endeavour were born. It's also why the Colosseum, the great cathedrals and pyramids exist. Each one of them started with a single thought. Each one of them was achieved because the imaginer believed. Every piece of matter on earth began with a thought. Become resilient to the realization of your thoughts. If you don't, no one else will. Your earnings, your creativity, your advancement and your riches all depend on your thoughts of possibility. Be willing to put more emphasis on your thoughts than hope alone would provide. Hope will not get you to where you want to be. Hope will limit your action. Hope should only occur with the hope of a thought. After the thought, move away from hope –

instead, move eagerly to welcome and embrace your abundance.

When your intentions are clear, and you are working toward your goals by acting in a specific way, your right to abundance is plentiful, indeed limitless.

True abundance is received when there is a constant balance between your mind and soul. Conflict may often arise, causing resistance between the two. When you act in a specific way toward your intentions, the harmony between the mind and soul will flourish. That symmetry gives permission for desire to enjoy acceptance for as long as it is genuine. As discussed in the previous chapter, your momentum of goodness will be carried out in all that you do, including the advancement of abundance.

As we also noted earlier, you must continue to flip traditional conditioned thinking upside down. If you allow entry to thoughts based on stereotypes of others or on societal influence as a whole, you will never break out of your conditioned mind. It is your right to go after what you desire. It is your right to find your unique personality. It is your right to believe in infinite possibility. It is your right to claim your abundance. And it is your right to realize your own power of being rich.

There are no limits to your wants and desires for as long as you continue to act in a specific way. Do not desire one thing at the expense of another. Do not fill your refrigerator simply to fill it. But fill it if you have a desire to feed the neighborhood. Do not manifest a yacht for it to sit outside of the water. Your desires should be in alignment with your need for empathetic action, right where you are. Actions otherwise could be construed as greed.

Continue to make your desire to be rich a clear and honest thought. Your desire will not materialize if it is in conflict. Therefore, you cannot at the same time have thoughts that go against your desire. Doing so will negate any and all progress toward your vision. If you desire to be rich and truly desire to be rich, accept nothing but thoughts and images of your desire to be rich.

Leave your mistakes, failures, and pitfalls in the past. Do not give them space in your mind. As you allow abundant thoughts, be cautious not to give any thought to anything less than abundance. If you were born into welfare, and a broken home and nothing but the clothes on your back, do not bring those thoughts into view. Leave those thoughts in the past. Don't fall into the trap of what Peter Sage calls "Let's blame our parents for everything." If you give an ounce of thought to anything contrary to your thoughts of abundance, your momentum will move downward in that contrary direction.

Be selective in the type of media you choose to engage. Be certain the public medium is complementary to your vision, so not to hinder your hard work. Should you find yourself in the company of such dialogue, stay proactive and limit your direct interaction. Certainly, do not participate in any nonsense in direct competition with your desires.

When you do speak of anything that may conflict with your desire, speak to it as advancing toward abundance of riches. Your intentions are meaningful even for those who may be in a moment of despair. Do not judge those, simply lift them up to a higher plane of spirit-stature.

Recognition

As you move toward your power of being rich, take time to recognize those around you. Lift them up to where you are. Pay genuine compliments to your family every single day. Tell your children how proud you are of them for simple acts they do. Teach them that you value them, appreciate them, and recognize all that they are doing to progress in their own right. Compliment your spouse every single day. Just like the rule of gratitude, hold a rule of recognition to those close to you. Take the utmost care of your core family. Nurture each one of them. Thank them constantly. Appreciate what they do and recognize their achievements. Help them in distress. Comfort them in sadness. Life certainly has its ups and downs and you must take firm hold when things fall off course. Tell your loved ones you love them. Hug them and show affection. Instill in them the confidence that they too can achieve anything that they put their mind to. Support them in their wants, needs, and desires. Allow them to explore. Help them see that they can manifest their goals. Teach them if they are open to that, but allow them to challenge and learn. No one man or woman is all-knowing. Keep an open mind.

Definition of Being Rich

We each have our own definition of being rich. The power of being rich is knowing just that—you hold your own power to live out your desires. I cannot dictate to, nor you to me, a compulsory definition of being rich. Your relationship with being rich depends on exactly where you are at this moment in time. Your relationship with the definition itself may change just as often as your place in time. Your definition of rich may be having a large family with lots of houses and material goods and worldly desires, whereas my definition of rich may be living in a modest home with less worldly desires. We both, however, can have simultaneous contentment in our mind, body, and spirit. In the end we both discovered the power of being rich and therefore embrace it as such. When it comes to creating wealth, or monetary value, or assets, your movement toward that desire is no different than the movement of any other desire. You must certainly act in a specific way in order to manifest and receive currency in the form of money. Money like all other desires is a form of energy, and you can move that energy toward you by using the same principles. All negative thoughts around money, including debt, bills, loss, scarcity, and lack cannot enter your mind. Money as an energy will come and flow through you, as with any other form of energy. You must keep that desire with you and remember to eliminate any stereotypes around the increase of money and begin to believe you will move toward acquiring whatever amount of money you wish to receive.

Keep in mind the laws of the universe. You cannot simply think of the money and expect you'll hit the lottery. Can it happen? Of course, but it's not likely. It is more likely that you frame your desired need of money and steadily work toward that need or want. You must act on it by taking action to acquire the money. The money will not miraculously show up in your bank account. What will happen, is that once you put your thoughts and intentions and desires in motion and work toward them, the money will flow to you in plentiful and unpredictable ways. Do not be concerned with how you will receive the money. Stay focused on your desire for the money and the good you will do for yourself and others with the money.

The currency of money also carries with it the universal laws that apply to everything mentioned in this book. That includes momentum when extreme and responsible action is taken.

"There's no such thing as work. There's activity you get paid for and activity you don't get paid for."

—David Meltzer

Allow your money to live as energy so that you are in tune with its vibration and frequency. Don't diminish its value as mere paper, or think of it as evil because it's what you need to survive. Flip it on its head. Utilize it as the energy that is necessary for you to fulfill your desire of being rich. It is not a means to an end, it is a means to your every desire. Nothing can flow without the exchange of money.

David Meltzer says, "There's no such thing as work. There's activity you get paid for and activity you don't get paid for." The day you begin to understand the energy associated with money is the day you'll fully appreciate that quote. When you love what you do, you will get compensated for what you do.

When you live in service, you don't expect to get paid for service. Both paid and unpaid service are activities, both are time spent. You will be more selective and responsible about the value you place on time. You will work toward getting paid for your unique abilities and you will be compensated by whatever means you choose.

"Riches are not from an abundance of worldly goods, but from a contented mind."

—Author Unknown

Chapter 10
Ultimate Richness

FULFILLMENT IS THAT OF WHAT OCCURS ON THE INSIDE; A FEELING OF ULTIMATE CONTENTMENT.

What is ultimate richness? Is there such a thing?

Indeed.

When your heart is rich, your mind is rich, and your soul is rich... you are, without any doubt, rich.

There is nothing I want in life that I cannot obtain, acquire or control. My richness is my happiness. My happiness outweighs worry, fear, anxiety, guilt, shame, ridicule, and anger. Each day, I remind myself of why I am rich. Each day I appreciate the power of being rich. Each day I make it a priority to help others see the greatness in themselves so they too can become rich.

Attaining ultimate richness means you have been able to successfully show yourself and those you serve that you have a complete belief in yourself and your unique abilities to influence and increase the growth of others.

Once you reach this place of fulfillment, you will have reached your innate power of being rich. Once you can show your transparent self, you will have reached the pinnacle level of attraction which will draw others to you in abundance. And as long as you continue to act in a specific way the momentum of your riches will multiply. You will no longer face fear or worry about pettiness, rather you will be on to accomplish bigger and better goals and desires. And as long as you continue to respect the universal laws and have a positive mind, along with faith, trust, and belief while holding gratitude in your heart, there will be nothing you can't achieve.

The higher power of God wants nothing more than to help you reach your most precious desires. But without action no desires can be reached. A healthy body and a healthy mind have been destined to do good work. It is up to you to take that first step.

As you receive riches into your life, receive them with love, joy, and grace just as you expressed gratitude for them before they came to you. The reception and acceptance of your gifts are as important as the gifts themselves. Hold each one as a treasure, but do not be stingy. Your abundance will accumulate if you treat it as the energy it is. Allow it to fulfill desires and to be plentiful.

In closing, show respect for your riches. Your riches may include loved ones, assets, wealth, property, belongings, savings, valuables, pets—or more intangibles such as peace, comfort, fulfillment, joy, love, vulnerability, expression, transparency, rituals, talents, desires, goals, dreams, and ambitions.

Take care of your things and be sure to always act in a specific way.

Now, I'll put it all out there for the world to see. Here is my secret for attaining the power of being rich. It is a growing and ever-changing list, but currently this is the list I recite each day. It is my formula and my personal benchmark for success. You need to come up with your own list to read each day. Make it a ritual and part of your daily routine. It will never get old if you keep it fresh and new.

I love myself.

I am awesome.

I have so much to offer the world.

I love my wife with all of my being.

I love my children with every inch of my soul.

I love my immediate family and accept each one as they are.

I love my extended family and all that they are.

I love my friends and all we offer each other.

I love my colleagues, their talents and workmanship.

I love people… all people of every culture, race and religion.

I love my community.

I choose not to judge anyone, or anything outside of my control.

I am the light.

I lead by example.

I do not dwell on my mistakes.

I service others.

I genuinely want to help as many people on earth as I can.

I love the world we are so blessed to live in.

I love sharing the stories of others.

I love giving people a voice and a platform to share.

I love learning something from everyone.

I love empowering people to become the best version of themselves.

I love helping people find their unique abilities.

I love being a connector.

I love seeing others prosper.

I will continue to learn something new each day.

I will continue to make myself accessible to others.

I will respect my time and the time of others.

I will continue to create.

I will continue to take ownership for my actions.

I will continue to be grateful and express my gratitude for all things good.

I will respect the universal laws and trust them because they are inflexible.

I will respect my body and the food and drink I choose to take in.

I will respect my mind and continue to feed it goodness.

I will respect my spirit and my soul and the creator of life itself, all that is here and all that is yet to come.

I started this book by talking about being able to manifest and create your own reality and I will end this book in the same way. But now you should have more tools than you did before reading this book. You are now armed with more ideas. And now, you can take everything that I've written and formulate your own rules to create your own reality. For example, your reality may have advisors that guide your decisions each day. They can be the smartest and most creative advisors that ever gathered together in a single room. Create your own board of advisors. My advisors are those I mentioned in the acknowledgments. Whether they know it or not, they help me make decisions each day. You see, you're not alone in your reality if you choose not to be alone. You can invite anyone to your meeting room that you desire.

Make this fun. Life is fun. It is full of opportunity and adventure. Don't get so stressed. In fact, there's nothing to stress about when you create the reality you embody. Love yourself, love those around you, be grateful for everything you have and everything that's yet to come. Love your future self. Forgive your old self. Live in the present. Forget the past. Manifest whatever you desire. Build momentum. Build wealth. Build a castle in the clouds. Create wonderful things. Dismiss perfection. Embrace abundance and you will enjoy... truly enjoy, *The Power of Being Rich!*

"Everything you need you already have. You are complete right now, you are a whole, total person, not an apprentice person on the way to someplace else. Your completeness must be understood by you and experienced in your thoughts as your own personal reality."

—Wayne Dyer

Made in the USA
Columbia, SC
06 June 2022

61406496R00080